THE
- ## UNABRIDGED,
- ## UNCENSORED,
- ## UNBELIEVABLE

Garfield®

BY: JIM DAVIS

BALLANTINE BOOKS • NEW YORK

Library of Congress Catalog Card Number: 86-90729

ISBN: 0-345-33772-7

Manufactured in the United States of America

First Edition: November 1986

10 9 8 7 6 5 4 3 2 1

6

SUSHI

13

14

SLIPPERY WHEN WET

17

21

BOING

25

GARFIELD WITH SHADES

GARFIELD WITH MINI BLINDS

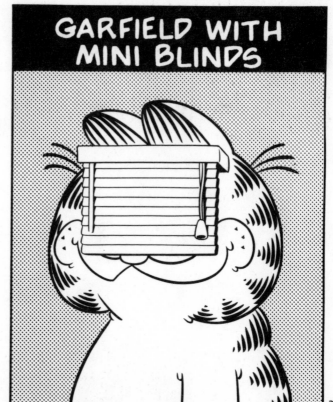

ONE OF THE DANGERS OF OVER-PETTING YOUR CAT

CATS OF THE WORLD

GERMANY

FRANCE

MEXICO

CANADA

35

ANCIENT EGYPTIAN MODE OF TRANSPORTATION FOR CATS:

CAT ON A HOT FUDGE SUNDAE:

CHEAP CAT TOUPEE:

STALKING THE WILD LEAF

53

CAT NIGHTMARE #47

54

scrit!

CAT CLAIMING ITS TERRITORY

DOGS... APPLY WITHIN
BEWARE OF DOG
TRESPASSERS WILL BE LICKED
ENTER AT YOUR OWN RISK

THINGS CATS SHOULDN'T SHARPEN THEIR CLAWS ON:

LITTLE KNOWN CAT FACTS

CATS HAVE
NINE LIVES

CROSS SECTION OF A DOG

CORNDOG

FURNITURE FOR CAT OWNERS

CHAIN MAIL CURTAINS

PLASTIC FLOWERS

ALUMINUM VASE

STAINLESS STEEL COUCH

LUCITE THROW RUG

ARMOR PLATED TABLE